The World's Most
Exotic Cars

John Martin

Capstone Press

M I N N E A P O L I S

Printed in the United States of America.

Capstone Press • 2440 Fernbrook Lane • Minneapolis, MN 55447

Editorial Director   John Coughlan
Managing Editor   John Martin
Copy Editor   Theresa Early
Editorial Assistant   Michelle Wood

Library of Congress Cataloging-in-Publication Data

Martin, John, 1968-
   The world's most exotic cars / John Martin
      p. cm.-- (Wheels)
   Includes bibliographical references and index.
   ISBN 1-56065-209-8 (lib. bdg.)
   1. Sports cars--Juvenile literature.   [1. Sports Cars.]
 I. Title. II. Series: Wheels (Minneapolis, Minn.)
TL236.M352 1995
629.222' 02--dc20   94-4714
                            CIP
                            AC

Table of Contents

Chapter 1   The World's Most Exotic Cars 5

Chapter 2   The Cars 17

Chapter 3   The Lamborghini Diablo 18

Chapter 4   The Dodge Viper RT/10 22

Chapter 5   The Vector W8 Twin Turbo 26

Chapter 6   The Corvette ZR-1 30

Chapter 7   The Acura NSX 34

Chapter 8   The Ferrari Testarossa 38

Glossary 43

To Learn More 45

Index 46

Chapter 1

The World's Most Exotic Cars

You are about to discover a group of sports cars known as "exotic cars."

Exotic means unfamiliar and unusual. The cars in this book are just that, and more. They are the ultimate sports cars.

It is easy to fall in love with exotic cars. Their rare beauty and awesome power draw you closer for a second look.

Although few people will ever be able to afford an exotic car, many find that learning about these amazing machines is the next best thing to driving one.

Whether made in Europe, Japan, or the United States, exotic cars share some traits. Their unusual shapes are strikingly beautiful. They can accelerate with breathtaking speed. Their gauges and gadgets seem to come straight out of a science fiction movie. Some of these rare and valuable cars are made at a rate of no more than a few dozen each year.

The Dodge Viper is the latest American-made exotic car.

Only 200 Vipers were made during 1992, the first year of production.

And they are fast! If there is one trait that attracts so many people to exotic cars, it is their speed. Some exotic cars can travel at a top speed of more than 200 miles (322 kilometers) per hour.

Good Looks

All exotic cars are sports cars, but not all sports cars are exotic cars. Once you have seen a few exotic cars, you will be able to recognize them at a single glance.

An exotic car has a more striking look than the everyday sports car. When developing an exotic car, companies spend millions of dollars to create a futuristic design that will catch people's eyes.

The Lamborghini Diablo

Handmade Cars

Most sports cars, even expensive ones, are made by machines on **production lines**. An exotic car, on the other hand, is the work of a craftsperson whose entire life has been committed to the creation of high-performance vehicles. This adds greatly to the value and quality of these machines.

Dodge uses small teams to assemble its exotic cars and to ensure quality.

Many of these craftspeople are the children and grandchildren of people who were themselves automobile craftspeople. They have a family commitment to the high standards of an exotic car.

Limited Production

To ensure the quality of the cars sold, manufacturers of exotic cars often limit the number of cars they make each year. This allows them to devote more time to each car and to assure buyers that the car will meet all expectations.

The highest production of an exotic car runs to only a few thousand. It is much more likely that only a few hundred or even a few dozen are made.

There are often more buyers for exotic cars than there are cars for sale. Even if you can

The Vector plant produces fewer than 20 cars per year.

afford an exotic car, you may have to join other hopeful buyers on a long waiting list.

Speed

Exotic cars offer the kind of speed that nearly makes your dream of flying come true. Some of these machines offer top speeds of more than 200 miles (322 kilometers) per hour, and most of the others let you go more than 150 miles (241 kilometers) per hour. The very thought of burning down the highway at such speed makes ordinary people into crazed exotic car lovers.

Chapter 2

The Cars

In the following pages are some of the most exotic cars available, together with information about their performance and **specifications**.

The specification information gives the volume of the car's **engine cylinders** in cubic centimeters (=cc). This number gives a good idea of how much power and speed a driver can get from a car's engine.

The engine of each car is shown as **V-6**, **V-8**, **V-10**, or **V-12**. This refers to the number of cylinders in the engine. Generally, the more cylinders a car has, the more power it can use for turning the wheels. The total power of the engine is measured in **horsepower** (=bhp).

Specifications
Engine: 5707 cc, V-12
Horsepower: 492 bhp
Price: $239,000

Chapter 3

The Lamborghini Diablo

Performance
Top speed: 202 miles (325 kilometers) per hour
1/4 mile: 13.3 seconds at 114 miles (183 kilometers) per hour

Acceleration
0-60 miles (0-96 kilometers) per hour: 4.5 seconds
0-100 miles (0-169 kilometers) per hour: 10.8 seconds

The Lamborghini Diablo

Lamborghini is an Italian exotic car maker with a great reputation. The company prides itself on the fine and careful craftsmanship that go into its cars.

The Diablo is a speed devil if there ever was one. Its mighty engine produces a lot of horsepower, and its sleek body helps cut the force of the wind.

The tapered hood of a sleek Lamborghini Diablo cuts the wind.

The Lamborghini Diablo is one of the heavier exotic cars.

Despite its sleek shape, the Diablo is a heavy car and drives like one. It can hold the road even at speeds greater than 200 miles per hour.

Many exotic car admirers think of the Lamborghini as the top make in exotic cars. For many of them, the Diablo is the best from Lamborghini.

Chapter 4

The Dodge Viper RT/10

Performance

Top speed: 160 miles (257 kilometers) per hour

1/4 mile: 13.1 seconds at 109 miles (175 kilometers) per hour

Acceleration

0-60 miles (0-97 kilometers) per hour: 4.8 seconds

0-100 miles (0-161 kilometers) per hour: 11.1 seconds

The Dodge Viper RT/10

Many people are calling the Viper the hottest American sports car to hit the road in years.

Dodge built only 200 Vipers during the first year of production in 1992. But the car drew so many admirers that Dodge immediately changed its plans. Ten times as many were made in 1993!

The Viper is built to perform. It handles

The interior of the Viper "wraps around" its passengers.

The Viper resembles the Shelby Cobra 427 of the 1960s.

beautifully with wide tires that grip the road well. The racing-style **suspension** system makes the car easier to control on the road.

The designers of the Viper wanted to build a car that resembled the "**muscle cars**" of the 1960s. The Shelby Cobra 427 was their model. They combined the best of the past with modern technology and ended up with one of the best cars ever made.

Specifications
Engine: 5973 cc, V-8
Horsepower: 625 bhp
Price: US$489,800

Chapter 5

The Vector W8 Twin Turbo

Performance
Top speed: 218 miles (351 kilometers) per hour
1/4 mile: 12.0 seconds at 124 miles (200 kilometers) per hour

Acceleration
0-60 miles (0-97 kilometers) per hour: 4.2 seconds
0-100 miles (0-161 kilometers) per hour: 8.3 seconds

The Vector W8 Twin Turbo

The engineers and craftspeople at Vector Aeromotive Corporation produce very few of these exotic cars.

You should think of a Vector W8 Twin Turbo as an aircraft. Aircraft materials and technology are used throughout. The instruments on the **dash board** are aircraft style, and the wiring is made to the specifications of military planes.

The Vector W8 Twin Turbo looks much like a jet fighter.

The rich leather interior of the Vector W8 Twin Turbo

This is a very low and wide car. There's plenty of leg room inside, and enough headroom for all but the tallest driver.

The Vector has plenty of luxuries. It has a leather **interior**, deep carpeting, and a great sound system.

The Vector does not come up short on performance, either. Its V-8 engine propels the car up to 218 miles (351 kilometers) per hour, making the Vector one of the fastest cars available.

Specifications
Engine: 5732 cc, V-8
Horsepower: 375 bhp
Price: US$68,960

Chapter 6

The Corvette ZR-1

Performance

Top speed: 178 miles (286 kilometers) per hour
1/4 mile: 13.9 seconds at 105 miles (169 kilometers) per hour

Acceleration

0-60 miles (0-97 kilometers) per hour: 5.6 seconds
0-100 miles (0-161 kilometers) per hour: 12.8 seconds

The Corvette ZR-1

The Corvette is the best-known sports car in the U.S. It has tens of thousands of fans.

While the Corvette is an exotic car, it is one you could use every day, rain or shine.

The shape of the Corvette, with its huge 17-inch (43-centimeter) wheels and tires, is admired by many exotic car buffs.

The Corvette performs well on both the track and in town. It handles well and rides smoothly.

The Chevrolet Corvette ZR-1 interior

The Corvette ZR-1 is an exotic car that many people use for day-to-day driving.

The ZR-1 is an optional high-performance version of the standard Corvette. Only 448 of them are made each year, and they cost twice the price of the basic model.

But the ZR-1 can do amazing things. It can, for example, go from 0 to 60 miles (0 to 97 kilometers) per hour in 4.8 seconds. That's less time than it takes for a telephone to ring three times!

Specifications
Engine: 2977 cc, V-6
Horsepower: 270 bhp
Price: US$68,600

Chapter 7

The Acura NSX

Performance

Top speed: 168 miles (270 kilometers) per hour
1/4 mile: 14.0 seconds at 103 miles (166 kilometers) per hour.

Acceleration

0-60 miles (0-97 kilometers) per hour: 5.8 seconds
0-100 miles (0-161 kilometers) per hour: 13.5 seconds

The Acura NSX

When the Acura NSX was introduced, it was the most expensive Japanese car in the U.S. But price did not keep demand down. Everybody loved it.

The Acura NSX has the engineering of a racer, the looks of an elegant sports car, and the usefulness of an ordinary passenger car.

The interior of the Acura NSX looks much like that of any ordinary passenger car.

The small V-6 in the NSX can still make 270 horsepower.

The NSX has a six-cylinder engine, while most exotic cars carry a V-8, V-10, or V-12. But the small engine does not slow down this speedster. It can reach a top speed of 168 miles (270 kilometers) per hour and go from 0 to 60 miles (0-97 kilometers) per hour in just 5.8 seconds.

Specifications

Engine: 4943 cc, V-12
Horsepower: 421 bhp
Price: US$189,000

Chapter 8

The Ferrari 512 Testarossa

Performance

Top speed: 192 miles (309 kilometers) per hour
1/4 mile: 12.9 seconds at 112 miles (180 kilometers) per hour.

Acceleration

0-60 miles (0-97 kilometers) per hour: 4.7 seconds
0-100 miles (0-161 kilometers) per hour: 10.5 seconds

The Ferrari 512 Testarossa

The Ferrari 512 Testarossa is definitely a luxury car. It comes with plush carpeting, deep leather seats, and full air conditioning.

But it's more than a mere luxury car. It's fast. It's easy to handle. It's quiet.

The quiet Ferrari 512 Testarossa

The interior of the Testarossa

This is not a small sports car. It's a wide and heavy two-seater. But the Testarossa accelerates quickly and handles easily.

For many people, the Italian-made Ferrari is the car of choice for performance and for great looks.

Glossary

acceleration–the rate of increase in the speed of a vehicle, usually measured in the time it takes to go from 0 to 60 or 100 miles per hour

dash board–the panel beneath the front windshield of a car

engine cylinder–a chamber in which exploding fuel moves a piston rapidly back and forth to generate power

horsepower–a measure of engine strength

interior–the inside compartment of a car, containing the dash board, seats, and controls

muscle car–a high-performance sports car

production line–a system of making a large number of cars in a short amount of time, using factory workers and robots for assembly

specification–a measurement of size, speed, or power

suspension–the system of springs, shock absorbers, and other parts that link the body of a car to its axles and wheels

turbo–a high-performance engine powered by mixing fuel and compressed air; or a "turbocharger," a supercharger driven by exhaust gases from the engine

V-6, **V-8**, **V-10**, **V-12**–engine sizes, named after the "V"-shaped arrangement of the cylinders.

To Learn More

Cruickshank, Gordon. *Million Dollar Autos*. Secaucus, NJ: Chartwell Books, Inc., 1992.

Flammang, James. *The Great Book of Dream Cars*. New York, NY: Beekman House, 1990.

Gabbard, Alex, and Graham Robson. *The World's Fastest Cars*. Lincolnwood, IL: Publications International, Ltd., 1989.

Hodges, David. *Inside 100 Great Cars*. Secaucus, NJ: Chartwell Books, Inc., 1988.

Italia, Bob. *Great Auto Makers and Their Cars*. Minneapolis, MN: The Oliver Press, 1993.

Stevenson, Sallie. *Sports Cars*. Mankato, MN: Capstone Press, 1991.

Index

acceleration, 8, 37, 41
  (*see also* specifications)
Acura NSX, 34-37
air conditioning, 40
aircraft technology, 28
assembly, 11-12
auto body, 20

buyers, 13

carpeting, 29, 40
Corvette ZR-1, 30-33
craftspeople, 11-12, 28
cylinders, 17

dash board, 28
design, 10, 28
designers, 25
Dodge, 12, 24
Dodge Viper, 8-9, 22-25

engine cylinder, 17
engines, 17 (*see also*
  specifications)
  V-6, 17, 37
  V-8, 17, 37
  V-10, 17, 37
  V-12, 17, 37

Ferrari Testarossa, 38-41

horsepower, 17, 20, 37
  (*see also* specifications)

interiors, 24, 29, 32, 36, 40-41

Lamborghini, 20-21
Lamborghini Diablo, 10, 18-21
leather, 29, 40
limited production, 12-13, 24, 28, 33

manufacturers, 12-13
muscle cars, 25

passengers, 24
price, 5, 15, 33, 36 (*see
    also* Specifications)
production costs, 10
production lines, 11

Shelby Cobra 427, 25
sound system, 29
speed, 9, 15, 17, 20-21,
    23, 27, 29, 37 (*see
    also* specifications)
specifications, 17
    Acura NSX, 34-35;
    Corvette ZR-1, 30-31;
    Dodge Viper RT/10,
    22-23;

Ferrari 512 Testa-
    rossa, 38-39;
    Lamborghini Diablo,
    18-19; Vector W8
    Twin Turbo, 26-27
suspension, 25

tires, 25, 32

Vector Aeromotive
    Corporations, 13, 28
Vector plant, 13
Vector W8 Twin Turbo,
    26-29

wheels, 17, 32
wind, 20
wiring, 28

Photo Credits:

Chrysler Motors: cover, pp. 4, 6-7, 9, 12, 16, 22-23, 25;
Road & Track: pp. 8, 10, 13, 14, 18-19, 20, 21, 24, 26-27,
28, 29, 30-31, 32, 33, 34-35, 36, 37, 38-39, 40, 41.